CANADA
WORLD ADVENTURES

BY HARRIET BRUNDLE

BookLife

©2017
Book Life
King's Lynn
Norfolk PE30 4LS

ISBN: 978-1-78637-191-1

Written by:
Harriet Bundle

Edited by:
Charlie Ogden

Designed by:
Gareth Liddington

A catalogue record for this book
is available from the British Library.

CANADA

WORLD ADVENTURES

CONTENTS

Words in **bold** can be found in the glossary on page 24.

WHERE IS CANADA?

Canada is in the **continent** of North America. It is next to the U.S.A. and is one of the biggest countries in the world.

CANADA

U.S.A

NORTH AMERICA

The **population** of Canada is over 35 million.
The capital city of Canada is called Ottawa.

Ottawa,
Canada

WEATHER AND LANDSCAPE

During the winter, the weather in Canada can be very cold and there is often lots of snow. The weather is usually warmer during the summertime.

Canada has a very wide range of different **landscapes**, including lakes, mountains and coastlines.

LAKE SUPERIOR, CANADA

Canada is home to thousands of lakes!

CLOTHING

The **indigenous** people of Canada are called Inuit. They wear animal skins and fur to help stay warm in the cold weather.

People in Canada usually wear comfortable and **modern** clothing.

RELIGION

A CHURCH IN CANADA

The religion with the most followers in Canada is Christianity. People who follow Christianity are called Christians.

Other people in Canada follow religions such as Islam, Hinduism and Buddhism. Many people in Canada do not follow any religion at all.

FOOD

POUTINE

Poutine is the **national** dish of Canada. It is made with French fries that are covered in gravy and cheese curd.

Maple syrup is also popular in Canada. This sweet sauce is often eaten with pancakes or waffles.

AT SCHOOL

Children in Canada start school when they are five years old and finish when they are eighteen.

Children in Canada are often encouraged to do activities outside of school, such as sport and art.

When there is snow, children can go skiing!

AT HOME

Most people in Canada live in towns and cities in the southern part of the country. This is because the weather is usually warmer in the south.

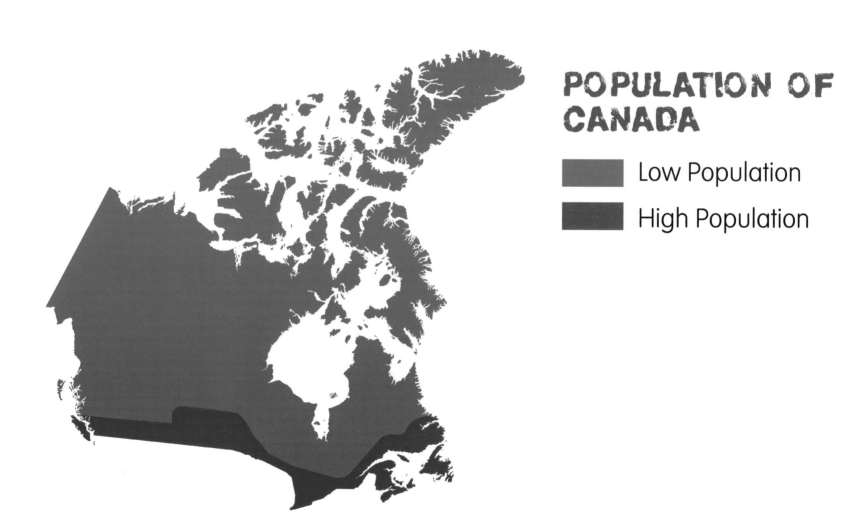

POPULATION OF CANADA

Low Population

High Population

Inuit used to live in igloos made of large blocks of ice that were tightly packed together in a dome shape.

IGLOO

FAMILIES

Parents and children usually live together in Canada and, in some cases, grandparents live with the family too.

In the past, families of Inuit lived together in groups. Between six and ten families would all live, work, hunt and eat together.

SPORT

The national winter sport of Canada is ice hockey. The sport involves two teams of six players and a small disk, called a puck, that each team tries to put in their opponents' net.

The national summer sport of Canada is lacrosse. The sport involves using a long racket with a net on the end to throw a ball into your opponents' net.

FUN FACTS

Canada has the longest coastline of any country in the world!

There are two main languages in Canada: French and English.

Canada is home to many amazing animals, such as cougars, wolves and moose.

GLOSSARY

continent	a very large area of land that is made up of many countries, like Africa and Europe
indigenous	originating from or naturally found in a particular place
landscapes	the physical features of different areas of land
modern	from present or recent times
national	relating to, characteristic of or common to a nation
population	the number of people living in a place

INDEX

Photocredits: Abbreviations: l-left, r-right, b-bottom, t-top, c-centre, m-middle. All images are courtesy of Shutterstock.com.

Front Cover – ANUCHA PONGPATIMETH, bg - Aleksey Klints. 2 – karamysh. 5 – Alex Papp. 6l – Popsidoodle. 6r - valleyboi63. 7 – Sorayot Chinkanjanarot. 8 – bikeriderlondon. 9 – Ivanko80. 10 – gvictoria. 11 – Zurijeta. 12 – bonchan. 13 – Magdalena Kucova. 14 – Poznyakov. 15 – Elena Elisseeva. 17 – Vova Shevchuk. 18 – Orange Line Media. 19 – Konstantin Shevtsov. 20 – Andrey Yurlov. 21 – James A Boardman. 22t – Sergey Lyashenko. 22bl – Stephen Finn. 23t – Brandy McKnight. 23m - Szczepan Klejbuk. 23b - Ghost Bear. Images are courtesy of Shutterstock.com. With thanks to Getty Images, Thinkstock Photo and iStockphoto.